BILL GATES

BY SARA GREEN

BELLWETHER MEDIA • MINNEAPOLIS, MN

Jump into the cockpit and take flight with Pilot books. Your journey will take you on high-energy adventures as you learn about all that is wild, weird, fascinating, and fun!

This edition first published in 2015 by Bellwether Media, Inc.

No part of this publication may be reproduced in whole or in part without written permission of the publisher. For information regarding permission, write to Bellwether Media, Inc., Attention: Permissions Department, 5357 Penn Avenue South, Minneapolis, MN 55419.

Library of Congress Cataloging-in-Publication Data

Green, Sara, 1964- author.
 Bill Gates / by Sara Green.
    pages cm. – (Pilot. Tech Icons)
 Summary: "Engaging images accompany information about Bill Gates. The combination of high-interest subject matter and narrative text is intended for students in grades 3 through 7"– Provided by publisher.
 Audience: Ages 7-12.
 Includes bibliographical references and index.
 ISBN 978-1-60014-987-0 (hardcover : alk. paper)
 1. Gates, Bill, 1955–Juvenile literature. 2. Microsoft Corporation–History–Juvenile literature. 3. Computer software industry–United States–Biography–Juvenile literature. 4. Businessmen–United States–Biography–Juvenile literature. I. Title.
 HD9696.2.U62G3746 2014
 338.7′610053092–dc23
                    2014006810

Printed in the United States of America, North Mankato, MN.

TABLE OF CONTENTS

CHAPTER 1

WHO IS BILL GATES?

Bill Gates helped make computers a part of people's everyday lives. He **co-founded** Microsoft, the world's largest personal computer **software** company. As **CEO**, he led the company to wild success. He became one of the most accomplished **entrepreneurs** on Earth. In 2013, Bill was worth more than $78 billion. This made him the world's richest person. However, he plans to give most of his money away through **philanthropy**. He co-founded the Bill & Melinda Gates **Foundation** with his wife. Together, they work to solve the world's biggest problems.

Bill was born on October 28, 1955, in Seattle, Washington. His father, William Gates Sr., was a lawyer. His mother, Mary, was a teacher. However, she stopped teaching to raise the family and **volunteer**. Bill has two sisters, Kristi and Libby. His grandmother also lived with the family. She helped raise Bill and his sisters. The family was very close. They enjoyed spending time together and often played games after dinner.

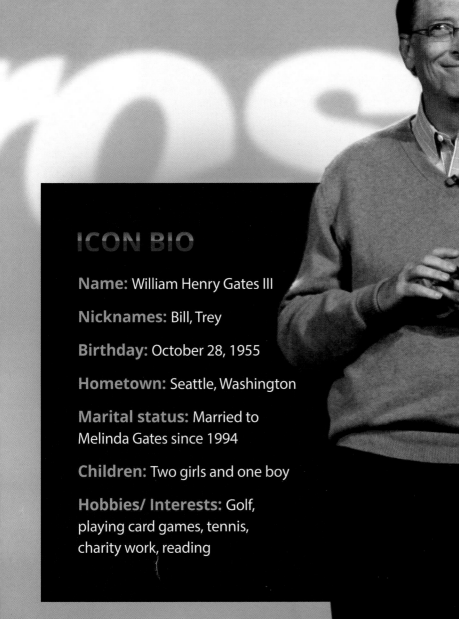

ICON BIO

Name: William Henry Gates III

Nicknames: Bill, Trey

Birthday: October 28, 1955

Hometown: Seattle, Washington

Marital status: Married to Melinda Gates since 1994

Children: Two girls and one boy

Hobbies/ Interests: Golf, playing card games, tennis, charity work, reading

5

CHAPTER 2

THE EARLY YEARS

Bill attended a public elementary school in Seattle. He was skilled in math and reading. However, other subjects bored him. He did not always pay attention to his teachers. This led to poor grades in some subjects. Bill's parents were concerned about his study habits. They decided to send him to a private school.

When Bill turned 13, he started at a school in Seattle called Lakeside. It was for boys in grades seven through twelve. The teachers pushed Bill to do his best. Soon, he was making friends and earning high grades. Most importantly, the school was one of the first to have access to a computer. This would change Bill's life forever.

A GIFTED PROGRAMMER

When Bill was a child, people did not have computers in their homes. Computers were so large that one would fill an entire room. However, a group of moms called the Lakeside Mothers' Club bought a computer terminal for the students to use. A phone line connected the terminal to a mainframe computer in downtown Seattle. The terminal fascinated Bill and his friends. They spent much of their free time learning how to use it. When Bill was in the eighth grade, he wrote his first program. It was a tic-tac-toe game that users played against the computer. However, computer time cost money. The Lakeside Mothers' Club provided some funds, but soon the money ran out.

Bill and his friends needed to find a way to pay for their own computer time. They had taught themselves valuable computer skills. They decided to use their skills to earn money. The boys started a computer business called the Lakeside Programmers Group.

THE FIRST SALE

Bill sold his first computer program when he was 17 years old. It was a class scheduling system. He sold it to his high school for $4,200.

"This is how I see the world, and it should make one thing clear: I am an optimist. But I am an impatient optimist."
— Bill Gates

The Lakeside Programmers Group soon received its first job. The Computer Center Corporation (CCC) in Seattle hired the boys to find **bugs**. They wanted to know why their computers **crashed**. In exchange, the boys received free computer time. But CCC went out of business in 1970. The Lakeside Programmers Group needed another job.

Word about these gifted young programmers had spread around Seattle. Soon another business hired them to write a **payroll** program. The programmers received computer time and pay for their work. When Bill was 15, he and his friend, Paul Allen, started a company called Traf-O-Data. They created and sold software that measured traffic flow in cities. The two earned $20,000 for their work. When Bill was a senior, a company called TRW hired him as a programmer. However, Bill would have to move to Vancouver, Washington, to work for them. Lakeside School gave Bill permission to leave while he was still a student. He received credit for his work at TRW as his senior project.

In the spring of 1973, Bill graduated from Lakeside School. That fall, he entered Harvard University in Cambridge, Massachusetts. He took a variety of classes, but he preferred to write computer programs. In the summer of 1974, he worked as a programmer with his friend, Paul.

Later that year, Paul showed Bill a magazine article about the first personal computer. The Altair 8800 was small enough to sit on a desk. A company in Albuquerque, New Mexico, called MITS made it. Bill was excited. He was certain that personal computers would change people's lives. Many tasks, such as typing and calculating numbers, would be easier. Bill saw an opportunity to help people and earn money. Bill and Paul did not have an Altair 8800. Even so, they spent two months writing a program for it. They traveled to New Mexico to try it out. It worked perfectly the first time they ran it! This was one of the first programs written for a personal computer.

A SUMMER IN WASHINGTON, D.C.

In the summer of 1972, Bill served as a congressional page in the U.S. House of Representatives.

CHAPTER 4

MICROSOFT

In 1975, MITS hired Bill and Paul to write programs for its personal computers. Bill took a break from Harvard and moved to New Mexico. There, Bill and Paul started a software company called Microsoft. Bill returned to Harvard for two semesters, but he was not content. In 1976, Bill left Harvard for good to focus on Microsoft.

In 1979, Bill moved Microsoft and its 13 employees to Washington. There, his leadership and business skills helped the company grow quickly. By the end of 1979, Microsoft had made over $2 million in sales. Soon, Microsoft was providing **operating systems** for personal computers all over the world. Today, the company has over 100,000 employees worldwide and earns more than $60 billion a year!

A FAMOUS NAME

The name Microsoft is a blend of the words *microcomputer* and *software*.

"Microsoft was founded with a vision of a computer on every desk, in every home. We've never wavered from that vision."
— Bill Gates

CHAPTER 5

CHANGING THE WORLD

In 1987, Bill met Melinda French at a Microsoft dinner. Melinda, a manager at Microsoft, was kind, confident, and intelligent. The two fell in love. In 1994, they got married in Hawaii. Today, they have two daughters and one son.

Together, Bill and Melinda started the Bill & Melinda Gates Foundation. This is one of the largest charitable foundations on Earth. It has already donated billions of dollars to improve lives around the world. Much of the money benefits healthcare and education in poor nations. This includes trying to stop deadly diseases. The foundation aims to reduce **poverty** and hunger, too. In the United States, many schools and public libraries also receive **grants**. Bill and Melinda have promised to donate most of their wealth to the foundation over time. This means they will continue to help people long into the future.

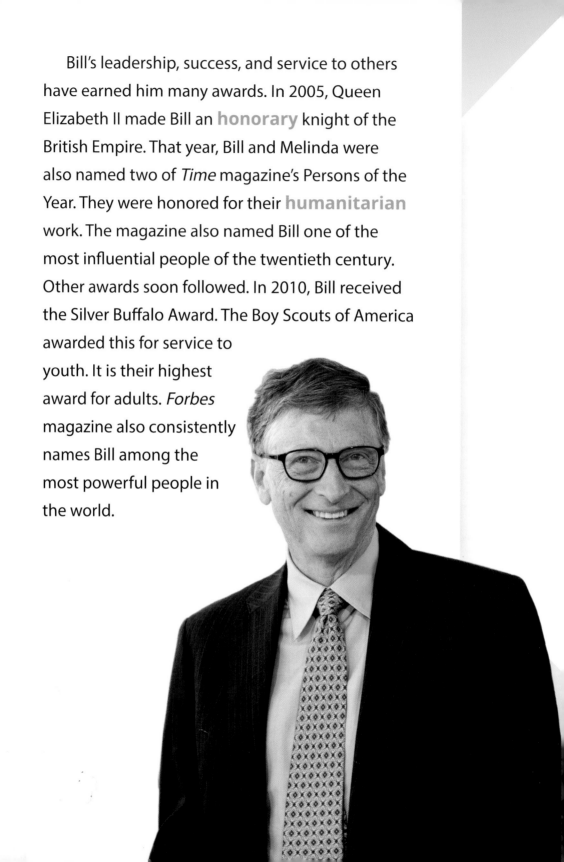

Bill's leadership, success, and service to others have earned him many awards. In 2005, Queen Elizabeth II made Bill an **honorary** knight of the British Empire. That year, Bill and Melinda were also named two of *Time* magazine's Persons of the Year. They were honored for their **humanitarian** work. The magazine also named Bill one of the most influential people of the twentieth century. Other awards soon followed. In 2010, Bill received the Silver Buffalo Award. The Boy Scouts of America awarded this for service to youth. It is their highest award for adults. *Forbes* magazine also consistently names Bill among the most powerful people in the world.

Today, Bill is no longer in charge of Microsoft. He stepped down in order to spend more time at the foundation. However, he continues to serve as an **advisor** to the new leader. In business and philanthropy, Bill is devoted to changing the world for the better.

RESUME

Education

1973-1976: Harvard University (Cambridge, Massachusetts)

1968-1973: Lakeside School (Seattle, Washington)

Work Experience

2008-present: Philanthropist

2000-2008: Chief Software Architect at Microsoft

1981-2014: Chairman of the Board of Directors for Microsoft

1981-2000: CEO of Microsoft

1977-1982: President of Microsoft

1975-1977: Computer programmer at MITS

Summer 1974: Computer programmer at Honeywell

Fall 1972-Spring 1973: Computer programmer at TRW

Community Service/Philanthropy

2013: Foundation awarded $8.1 million in grants to global health programs

2010: Foundation pledged $10 billion for vaccine research

2000: Signed the Giving Pledge; pledged to give away 95% of wealth

LIFE TIMELINE

January 1, 1979:
Microsoft headquarters now in Bellevue, Washington

Microsoft

Fall 1973:
Enters Harvard University in Cambridge, Massachusetts

October 28, 1955:
Born William Henry Gates III in Seattle, Washington

April 4, 1975:
Founds Microsoft with Paul Allen

1967-1973:
Attends Lakeside School in Seattle

Early 1975:
Writes first software program for the Altair personal computer

January 1977:
Moves to Albuquerque, New Mexico, to focus on Microsoft

December 2005:
Bill and Melinda are named two of *Time* magazine's Persons of the Year

February 4, 2014:
Steps down as chairman of Microsoft

November 20, 1985:
Microsoft releases Windows to the public

January 13, 2000:
Resigns as CEO of Microsoft and becomes Chief Software Architect

June 2007:
Receives honorary degree from Harvard University

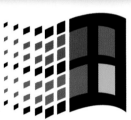

January 1, 1994:
Marries Melinda French

2000:
The Bill & Melinda Gates Foundation is formed

June 27, 2008:
Retires from day-to-day duties at Microsoft to work full-time at the foundation

1987:
Becomes the youngest billionaire ever

BILL & MELINDA GATES *foundation*

March 2014:
Ranked number one on *Forbes'* list of the world's billionaires

March 2, 2005:
Knighted by Queen Elizabeth II

GLOSSARY

advisor—a person who gives advice

bugs—mistakes in computer programs

CEO—Chief Executive Officer; the CEO is the highest-ranking person in a company.

co-founded—founded a company with one or more people

crashed—stopped working

entrepreneurs—people who start businesses

foundation—an institution that gives money to charitable organizations

grants—money given to a person or organization for a special purpose

honorary—given as a sign of honor or achievement

humanitarian—a person who seeks to improve the welfare of other people

mainframe—a very large, powerful computer

operating systems—the main programs in computers that control the way they work; operating systems make it possible for other computer programs to function.

payroll—a list of a company's employees and the amount of money they are paid

philanthropy—giving time and money to help others

poverty—the state of being poor

software—a program that tells a computer what to do

terminal—an electronic machine people enter data into; a terminal connects to a computer.

volunteer—to do something for others without expecting money in return

TO LEARN MORE

AT THE LIBRARY

Demuth, Patricia. *Who Is Bill Gates?* New York, N.Y.: Grosset & Dunlap, 2013.

Gregory, Josh. *Bill and Melinda Gates*. New York, N.Y.: Children's Press, 2013.

Lesinski, Jeanne M. *Bill Gates: Entrepreneur and Philanthropist*. Minneapolis, Minn.: Twenty-First Century Books, 2009.

ON THE WEB

Learning more about Bill Gates is as easy as 1, 2, 3.

1. Go to www.factsurfer.com.

2. Enter "Bill Gates" into the search box.

3. Click the "Surf" button and you will see a list of related web sites.

With factsurfer.com, finding more information is just a click away.

INDEX